HOME REMEDY

Publications International, Ltd.

Front Cover: Art Explosion Collection

Contributing Illustrators: Jeff Moores, Bot Roda

Louis Weber, CEO
Publications International, Ltd.
7373 North Cicero Avenue
Lincolnwood, Illinois 60712

Permission is never granted for commercial purposes.

ISBN-13: 978-1-4127-1499-0
ISBN-10: 1-4127-1499-0

Manufactured in China.

8 7 6 5 4 3 2 1

CONTENTS

PRACTICE COMMONSENSE CARE AT HOME

It's extremely frustrating to be sick these days. You go to the doctor's office, only to wait 45 minutes past your scheduled appointment because it's so busy. You get a prescription for a drug with a name you can't pronounce, let alone remember, and then you have to wait for a pharmacist to explain how it's going to interact with the three other prescriptions you're taking. And the frustration of trying to figure out what your health insurance will pay for makes you even sicker.

Maintaining your health can be easier. You can safely and effectively treat many common ailments at home, sometimes at little or no cost. The home remedies we offer here aren't miracle cures; they're commonsense approaches to manage nagging symptoms. Of course, some conditions require professional care, so if you're in doubt, see your doctor.

COMMON PROBLEMS

No matter where you live, how old
you are, or whom you hang out
with, you're at risk for catching a
cold or the flu. And if you're
around someone with a sore
throat, the odds are pretty good
that scratchy, painful fiend is going
to find its way to you. Even if you
take great care to stay away from those
who carry the virulent bugs that cause
these ailments, you might be one of the
millions of people who wage a war against allergies.
The fact is that we're all under constant attack from
everyday illnesses, but that doesn't mean we have to
be miserable, especially when there are simple home
remedies that provide relief.

Allergies

For many people, each change of season brings its
own brand of allergy triggers and irritants. In cases of
common hay fever and allergies, these pollutants can
bring on symptoms that range from a continuous,
annoying postnasal drip to a full-scale, coughing-
sneezing-itchy-eyed allergy attack. Other allergy sufferers, such as those with allergic asthma or an allergy
to bee stings, can die from attacks. The following tips

are designed to help reduce the discomfort caused by the most common allergies. They may be used in combination with an allergist's treatment or, if your allergies are mild, by themselves.

Rinse your eyes. If your eyes are itchy and irritated and you have no access to allergy medicine, rinsing them with cool, clean water can be soothing. Although not as effective as an antihistamine, this remedy certainly can't do any harm.

Try a warm washcloth. Do your sinus passages feel congested and painful? A washcloth soaked in warm water may make things flow a little easier. Place the washcloth over the nose and upper-cheek area, and relax for a bit.

Say hello to saline. Irrigating the nose with saline solution (salt water) may help soothe upper respiratory allergies by removing irritants that become lodged in the nose and cause inflammation. In fact, saline solution may even wash away some of the inflammatory cells themselves. You can buy saline solution at your local drugstore, or you can make your own fresh solution daily by mixing a teaspoon of salt and a pinch of baking soda in a pint of warm, distilled water. Bend over a sink and sniff a bit of solution into one nostril at a time, allowing it to drain back out through the nose or mouth; do this once or twice a day. (If you also have asthma, however, check with your doctor before trying this remedy.)

Wash your hair. If you've spent long hours outdoors during the pollen season, wash your hair to remove pollen after you come inside. The sticky yellow stuff tends to collect on the hair, making it more likely to fall into your eyes.

Take a shower. If you wake up in the middle of the night with a coughing, sneezing allergy attack, a hot shower may help by removing any pollen residues you've collected on your body throughout the day. (You might want to change your pillowcase, too.) There's also a good chance your sinuses will open up, at least for a while, making breathing a little easier. The warm water may even help you relax and go back to sleep.

Protect your peepers. On a windy day during pollen season, a pair of sunglasses (or your regular prescription eyeglasses, if you wear them) can help shield your eyes from airborne allergens. For extra protection, try a pair of sunglasses with side shields or even a pair of goggles.

Shut the windows. A fresh breeze blowing through an open window on a spring day may sound inviting, but it's bad news for an allergy sufferer, because pollen can fill the house. Keep windows closed at all times to minimize contact with the powdery stuff.

Go bare. Carpets are a notorious haven for dust mites, which are microscopic bugs that feed on the dead skin cells we constantly shed; dust-mite droppings spur allergies in millions of people. Bare floors that are vacuumed and damp-mopped frequently will help keep down your home's dust-mite population (you can't get rid of them all). If you can't remove all the carpeting in your home, at least opt for bare floors in your bedroom. Studies show the bedroom harbors more dust mites than any other room in the home, and you probably spend about a third of every day there.

Filter your vacuum. When you can't remove carpets, keeping them as clean as possible will help you breathe a bit easier. But beware: Many vacuums blast small particles of dust back into the air, leaving behind plenty of allergens to keep you sneezing and wheezing. Use a vacuum that has a built-in HEPA (high-efficiency particulate air) filter or attach a filter to the exhaust port of your canister vacuum (uprights usually don't have an exhaust port). If dust really bothers you and you have the money, consider investing in an industrial-strength vacuuming system. Speak with your allergist to find out whether such products are appropriate for you and where you can purchase filters or special vacuums.

Dust with a damp cloth. Dusting at least once a week is important, but if done improperly, it may aggravate respiratory allergies. Avoid using feather dusters, which tend to spread dust around; instead, control dust with a damp cloth. Dusting sprays may give off odors that can worsen allergies. If dusting really bothers you, don't do it. Ask a spouse or family member to do the dirty work, or hire a housekeeper, if possible.

Dehumidify. Dust mites love a humid environment because it allows them to reproduce like crazy. Invest in a de-humidifier or use an air conditioner, which works equally well. A dehumidifier can also help prevent mold, another allergen, from growing (just be sure to follow the manufacturer's maintenance instructions). And use the exhaust fan when cooking or showering to keep humidity to a minimum.

Wash your pet. Fido and Fifi produce allergy-causing substances in their sweat and saliva that get on their fur. Fortunately, these allergens dissolve in water, so a warm bath can rinse away the problem. If you're a cat owner and can't imagine bathing your beloved feline for fear of nearly being scratched to death, take heart: Some cats (though a minority, to be sure) purr when bathed. If you start bathing your feline regularly when it's a kitten, chances are better

that clean-up time will be a harmonious experience. Wash your cat in warm water, with no soap, once every other week. In addition, try to wash your hands soon after you've had direct contact with your furry friend.

Is It a Food Allergy?

Do you feel congested after you eat dairy products? Does red meat make you feel sluggish? Does sugar give you a headache? If you answered "yes" to any of these questions, you probably *don't* have a food allergy.

Many people confuse food allergies with food intolerances. While the latter can trigger unpleasant symptoms such as those described above, true food allergies can be extremely serious—even deadly.

If you are truly allergic to a food, the reaction will be almost immediate, occurring from within a few minutes to two hours after you eat it. The most common symptoms are hives, diffuse swelling around the eyes and mouth, or abdominal cramps. A less common symptom is difficulty breathing. In severe cases, extremely low blood pressure, dizziness, or loss of consciousness may result. In these instances, emergency medical attention is required.

Common Cold

Most people know the symptoms of the common cold all too well. A cold is an upper respiratory infection caused by any one of hundreds of different viruses. The symptoms you experience as a cold are actually the body's natural immune response. In fact, by the time you feel like you're coming down with a cold, you've likely already been infected for a day and a half. Although Americans spend billions of dollars annually on doctor visits and cold remedies, there is no cure. Still, there are things you can do to feel better.

Rest. First and foremost, you should take it easy because your body is spending a lot of energy fighting off the cold virus. Staying away from work is probably a good idea too, from a prevention standpoint; coworkers will appreciate your not spreading the cold virus around the workplace.

Drink up. Nonalcoholic fluids may help thin the mucus, thus keeping it flowing freely and making it easier for the body to expel. When mucus is ousted, so are the viral particles making you sick that are trapped within it. Water and other liquids also combat dehydration. Drink at least eight ounces of fluid every two hours.

Cook up some chicken soup. One of the most beneficial hot fluids you can consume when you have a cold is chicken soup. Moses Maimonides, a physician and rabbi, first prescribed chicken soup for the common cold in twelfth-century Egypt and it has been a favorite folk remedy ever since. In 1978, Marvin Sackner, M.D., of Mount Sinai Hospital in Miami Beach, Florida, included chicken soup in a test of the effects of sipping hot and cold water on the clearance of mucus. To the doctor's surprise, chicken soup placed first, hot water second, and cold water a distant third. Physicians aren't sure exactly why chicken soup helps clear nasal passages, but many agree "it's just what the doctor ordered."

Use a saltwater wash. Molecules your body makes to fight infection called cytokines, or lymphokines, cause the inflammation and swelling in your nose when you have a cold. Research has shown that washing away  these molecules can reduce swelling. Fill a clean nasal-spray bottle with diluted salt water (one level teaspoon salt to one quart water), and spray into each nostril three or four times. Repeat five to six times per day.

Gargle with warm salt water. Gargling with warm salt water (¼ teaspoon salt in four ounces warm water) every one to two hours can soothe a sore, scratchy

Make the Right Call

Although colds can be effectively treated at home, you should call your doctor if

- You have a headache and stiff neck with no other cold symptoms. (Your symptoms may indicate meningitis.)
- You have a headache and sore throat with no other cold symptoms. (It may be strep throat.)
- You have cold symptoms and significant pain across your nose and face that doesn't go away. (You may have a sinus infection, which could require antibiotics.)
- You have a fever above 101 degrees Fahrenheit (adults) and the aspirin or other fever-reducer you've taken hasn't brought it down.
- Your child has a fever above 102 degrees Fahrenheit.
- Your cold symptoms seem to be going away but you suddenly develop a fever. (It may indicate pneumonia, which is more likely to set in toward the end of a cold.)
- You have a "dry" cough—one that doesn't bring up phlegm—for more than ten days.
- You cough up blood.

throat. Salt water is an astringent (meaning it causes tissue to contract), which can soothe inflammation in the throat and may help loosen mucus.

Vaporize it. The steam from a vaporizer can loosen mucus, especially if the mucus has become thick and gunky. A humidifier will add moisture to your immediate environment, which may make you feel more comfortable and will keep your nasal tissues moist. That's helpful because dry nasal membranes provide poor protection against viral invasion. If you don't have a vaporizer, you can drape a towel over your head and bend over a pot of boiled water—just be careful not to burn yourself.

Fever

Fever is not a disease in itself but simply a symptom of some other condition, usu-ally an infection caused by a bacterium or virus. When such an enemy invades, white blood cells attack, releasing a substance called pyrogen. When pyrogen reaches the brain, it signals the hypothalamus, a tiny structure at the base of the brain that regulates the body's temperature, to set itself at a higher point. If that new set point is higher than 100 degrees Fahrenheit, you have a fever. When a fever develops, what should you do? Try the advice that follows.

Don't force yourself under cover. Shivers are your body's way of creating heat to boost your temperature, so if your teeth are chattering or you feel chilled, by all means, cover up to make yourself more comfortable. However, once your fever is established and you start feeling hot, bundling yourself under a pile of blankets will only hold in the heat and likely make you feel worse. You can't "sweat out a fever," or get a fever to break by forcing your body temperature up even higher. So if you feel as though you're burning up, toss off those covers or use a single, light sheet.

Undress. With your body exposed as much as possible, your sweat glands will be better able to release moisture, which will make you feel more comfortable. Strip down to your skivvies—that means a diaper for an infant and underpants and thin undershirt for an older child or adult.

Dip. Sponge yourself with tepid water or, better yet, sit in a tub of cool water (though definitely not ice-cold water, because that can induce shock) for half an hour. If you put a feverish child in a tub or sink of water, be sure to hold him or her. Don't apply an alcohol rub, because it can be absorbed into the skin and cause alcohol poisoning.

Sip. Fever, especially one accompanied by vomiting or diarrhea, can lead to fluid loss and an electrolyte imbalance, so it's important to keep drinking. Cool water is best, but unsweetened juices are okay if that's what tastes good. Getting a child to drink plenty of water is sometimes difficult, so try Popsicles or flavored ices that are made primarily of water.

Let it run. Bear in mind that fever-reducing drugs (antipyretics) are designed to make you feel more comfortable during the course of a fever. The fact is, however, that fever may do an ailing body some good by making it less hospitable to the infecting organism, so you may want to let it run its course rather than rushing to bring it down with medications. An untreated fever in an adult or a child older than six months of age tends to be self-limited, relatively benign, and unlikely to escalate to the point that it causes harm. Letting a fever run its course is not the best idea for everyone, however. Seek medical advice immediately for:

- An infant younger than two months of age with a rectal temperature of 100.2 degrees Fahrenheit or higher (or lower than 95 degrees)

- A child two months of age or older with a rectal temperature of at least 102 (or, in an older child, an oral temperature of at least 101)

- A child two months of age or older with a rectal temperature between 100 and 102 (or, in an older child, an oral temperature between 99 and 101) that is accompanied by unexplained irritability; listlessness or lethargy; repeated vomiting; severe headache, stomachache, or earache; croupy "barking" cough; or difficulty breathing

- Any fever that lasts more than one day in a child younger than two years of age or more than three days in a child two years old or older

- A pregnant woman with any above-normal body temperature (generally 100 degrees or higher)

- An otherwise healthy adult with a temperature higher than 104 (oral); a temperature of 102 (oral) or higher accompanied by a serious underlying illness, such as heart arrhythmia or lung disease; or a temperature of 100 or higher that lasts for more than three days or is accompanied by severe headache, neck pain or stiffness, chest or abdominal pain, swelling of the throat or difficulty breathing, skin rash, sensitivity to bright light, confusion or unexplained irritability, listlessness, repeated vomiting, pain during urination, or redness or swelling of the skin

If a fever is making you or your child very uncomfortable, you can use a nonprescription antipyretic. Aspirin, ibuprofen, and acetaminophen are all antipyretics. Aspirin and ibuprofen also have an anti-inflammatory action, which can be an advantage in certain conditions, such as an abscess, that may cause fever. However, do not give aspirin products to children younger than 19 years of age because of the risk of a potentially fatal condition known as Reye's syndrome; stick with acetaminophen for children. Follow all package directions carefully.

Influenza

Although "the flu" has become a catchall term for any affliction of the upper respiratory tract (and is also often improperly used for infections of the gastrointestinal tract), the condition it refers to—influenza—is a specific viral infection that strikes every year, typically between October and April. Your best defense against the flu is to be vaccinated, but because flu strains change every year, no vaccination is going to be 100 percent effective. Regardless of the strain, the symptoms are generally the same: high fever, sore throat, dry cough, severe muscle aches and pains, fatigue, and loss of appetite. Some people even experience pain and stiffness in the joints. If you don't manage to avoid this relentless bug, you can do a few things to ease some of the discomforts and help your body fight back.

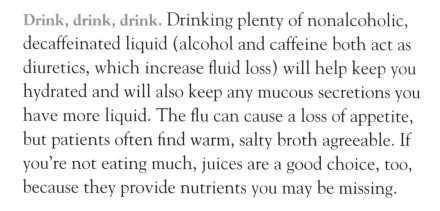

Rest up. Plan on sleeping and relaxing for a few days. Consider the flu a good excuse to take a needed break from the daily stresses of life. If you absolutely must continue to work, at least get to bed earlier than usual and try to go into the office a little later in the morning.

Drink, drink, drink. Drinking plenty of nonalcoholic, decaffeinated liquid (alcohol and caffeine both act as diuretics, which increase fluid loss) will help keep you hydrated and will also keep any mucous secretions you have more liquid. The flu can cause a loss of appetite, but patients often find warm, salty broth agreeable. If you're not eating much, juices are a good choice, too, because they provide nutrients you may be missing.

Humidify your home in winter. Part of the reason the flu tends to strike in the colder months is your furnace. Artificial heat lowers humidity, and a dry environment allows the influenza virus to thrive. (Colder outside air also pushes people together in confined indoor spaces, making it easier for the flu bug to spread.) Adding some moisture to the air in your home with a warm- or cool-mist humidifier during the winter may not only help prevent the spread of flu, it may also make you feel more comfortable if you do get it.

Suppress a dry cough. You can reach for over-the-counter relief for a dry, hacking cough that's keeping you from getting the rest you need. When shopping for a cough remedy, look for a product that contains the cough suppressant dextromethorphan.

Encourage a "productive" cough. A cough that brings up mucus, on the other hand, is considered productive and should generally not be suppressed with cough medicines. Drinking fluids will help bring up the mucus of a productive cough and will ease the cough a little, as well.

Sore Throat

A sore throat can be a minor, but annoying, ailment, or it can be a symptom of a serious illness. Causes range from a stuffy nose or a cold to strep throat. Because untreated strep throat can lead to rheumatic fever and scarlet fever, it's important to get medical help as early as possible. Along with producing severe soreness in your gullet, strep throat may be accompanied by fever, body aches and pains, and

An Old-Fashioned Sore-Throat Tonic

The following came from a book of home remedies published more than 130 years ago. Some doctors still swear the tonic is surprisingly palatable and works wonders. (Do not give it or any other honey-containing food or beverage to children younger than two years of age. Honey can carry a bacterium that can cause a kind of food poisoning called infant botulism and may also cause allergic reactions in very young children.)

- One tablespoon honey, any kind
- One tablespoon vinegar, preferably apple-cider vinegar
- Eight ounces hot water

Mix all the ingredients together in a mug and sip slowly (but don't let it get cold). Use as often as desired.

malaise. If you have these symptoms, or if you have a sore throat that lasts more than two or three days, see a doctor. For mild sore throats that accompany a cold or allergy, the tips below may help ease your discomfort.

Gargle with warm salt water. Make a saline solution by adding ½ teaspoon salt to a cup of very warm water. Gargling with this fluid can help soothe a sore throat.

Gargle with Listerine. Another good gargling fluid is the mouthwash Listerine. If you share the product with anyone else in your household, don't drink straight from the bottle; instead, pour a small amount into a cup.

Drink hot liquids. Coating the tissue in your throat with warm liquid, such as coffee, tea, or hot lemonade. Hot liquids soothe the inflamed membranes in the thoat that are the source of your pain.

Take it easy. Common sense dictates staying in bed or at least resting when a sore throat has you down. You'll have more energy to fight the infection.

Suck on hard candy. Some doctors say sugar can help soothe a sore throat and the ticklish cough that may come with it. If nothing else, sucking on hard candy, even the sugar-free kind, can help keep your mouth and throat moist, which will make you feel more comfortable.

Steam it out. One old-fashioned remedy for a cold or sore throat is a steam tent—sitting with your face over a bowl of steaming hot water and your head covered with a towel to keep in the steam. Several scientific studies have shown that steaming can shorten the duration of a throat infection.

Keep the fluids coming. Drink as much fluid as you can—at least eight to ten 8-ounce glasses per day. Keeping your throat well-lubricated with soothing liquids can prevent it from becoming dry and irritated and may even help banish the infection faster.

ACHES & PAINS

If something hurts, you're not likely to perform the action that causes the pain. How many times does it take to convince you not to put your hand on a hot stove-top burner? However, when you're talking about arthritis, back pain, head-aches, or muscle pain trig-

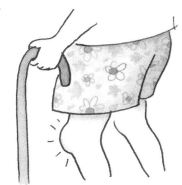

gered by simple movements, exercise, or even reading or using a computer, you're dealing with serious qual-ity-of-life issues. You don't have to be imprisoned by the pain—there are simple ways to alleviate it or avoid it in the first place, and they don't involve pop-ping more pills.

Arthritis

According to the Arthritis Foundation, an estimated 46 million Americans are caught in the grip of some form of arthritis or joint problem. And few of us will make it to a ripe old age without joining the fold. If one of these diseases has a painful hold on you, read on. Although there are no cures, there are steps you can take to ease discomfort and get back more control over your life.

Easing Stiffness and Discomfort

Here are some tips to help relieve discomfort and get you back into the swing of things.

Keep moving. Be as active as you can to keep your joints functioning as long as possible. Even everyday activities, such as walking, gardening, and housecleaning, can help your joints, as can range-of-motion, aerobic, and resistance exercises. Talk with your doctor or physical therapist about the best exercises for you.

Play in a pool. A heated pool or whirlpool may be the perfect environment for exercise (unless you are pregnant, in which case you should avoid heated whirlpools and hot tubs, or have other chronic health problems, in which case you should get your doctor's approval first). Try a few simple exercises while in the water. The buoyancy will help reduce the strain on your joints. Warm water helps loosen joints and makes muscles more pliable. In a pinch, a hot shower may do: Running the stream of water down your back, for instance, may help relieve back stiffness and discomfort.

Put on a scarf. Not around your neck, but around the elbow or knee joint when it aches. The added warmth may bring some relief, but be careful not to wrap it too tightly.

Pull on a pair of stretch gloves. The tightness may help reduce the swelling in arthritic fingers, and the warmth created by covered hands may make the joints feel better. Wearing thermal underwear may help, too.

Get "down." Goose down blankets warm up the joints and help ease pain. If you're allergic to down, try an electric blanket.

Osteoarthritis vs. Rheumatoid Arthritis

There are more than 100 different forms of arthritis, but the two most widely known are osteoarthritis and rheumatoid arthritis. Osteoarthritis is by far the most common form.

Osteoarthritis is primarily marked by a breakdown and loss of joint cartilage. Cartilage is the tough tissue that separates and cushions the bones in a joint. As cartilage is worn away and the bones begin to rub against each other, the joint becomes irritated. In osteoarthritis, this breakdown of cartilage is accompanied by minimal inflammation, hardening of the bone beneath the cartilage, and bone spurs (growths) around the joints. Most people develop some osteoarthritis as they age.

Rheumatoid arthritis, on the other hand, is not an inevitable aspect of the aging process. For unknown reasons, the synovial membrane, or lining, of a joint becomes inflamed, resulting in pain, swelling, heat, and redness.

Watch your weight. Being overweight puts more stress on the joints. In fact, a weight gain of 10 pounds puts the equivalent of 40 extra pounds of stress on the knees.

Protecting Your Joints

In addition to easing discomfort, you can learn to live well with arthritis by protecting your joints. Here are some helpful tips from the Arthritis Foundation.

Spread the strain. As a general rule, you want to avoid activities that involve a tight grip or that put too much pressure on your fingers. For example, use the palms of both hands to lift and hold cups, plates, pots, and pans, rather than gripping them with your fingers or with only one hand.

Avoid holding one position for a long time. Keeping joints "locked" in the same position for any length of time will only add to your stiffness and discomfort. Relax and stretch your joints as often as possible.

"Arm" yourself. Whenever possible, use your arm instead of your hand to carry out an activity. For example, push open a heavy door with the side of your arm rather than with your hand and out-stretched arm.

Replace doorknobs and round faucet handles with long handles. They require a looser, less stressful grip (or no grip at all) to operate, so you'll put less strain on your joints.

Build up the handles on your tools. For a more comfortable grip, look for household tools, utensils, and writing implements that have chunky, padded handles. Or tape a layer or two of thin foam rubber, or a foam rubber hair curler, around the handles of brooms, mops, rakes, spatulas, knives, pens, and pencils.

Let automatic appliances do the work for you. Electric can openers and knives, for instance, are easier to operate than manual versions. An electric toothbrush has a wider handle than a regular toothbrush.

Let loose with loops. You won't need quite as tight a grip if you put loops around door handles, such as those on the refrigerator and oven. Have loops sewn on your socks, too, and then use a long-handled hook to help you pull them up.

Contact the Arthritis Foundation. Learn about all kinds of joint-friendly or energy-saving items specially made for people with arthritis by contacting the Arthritis Foundation. Call 800-568-4045 or visit the organization's Web site at www.arthritis.org.

Back Pain

Almost every American suffers from back pain at some point in his or her life. The good news is that by following some simple steps, you can be feeling better in just a few days. Additionally, you can help ensure that you won't have to endure similar discomfort in the future.

Easing the Pain

The following remedies are appropriate for anyone who is suffering from back pain due to tight, aching muscles or a strain. However, if you are experiencing pain, weakness, or numbness in the legs, or a loss of bowel or bladder control, see a doctor right away.

Don't take it lying down. Mounting research shows that lying down for an extended period not only fails to speed up relief of lower back pain but it also may make it even worse. If you feel you must rest your aching back, the best position is lying flat on your back with two pillows underneath your knees. Never lie facedown, because this position forces you to twist your head to breathe and might cause neck pain. Any more than three days of bed rest could weaken the muscles and make them more prone to strain.

Ice it. Applying an ice pack to the painful area within 24 hours of an injury can help keep inflammation to a minimum and ease discomfort by decreasing the ability of nerves to send pain signals to the brain. Place a thin towel on the painful area, then apply the ice pack on top of the towel. Leave the pack on for 20 minutes, take it off for 30 minutes, and then replace it for another 20 minutes.

Take a hot bath. If more than 24 hours have passed since the injury occurred, ice will not help reduce pain or inflammation. After that first day, heat may help increase the elasticity of the muscles some-what, so try soaking in a tub of hot water for 20 minutes or more. Pregnant women, however, should not sit in a hot bath or hot tub for too long, because raising the body temperature over 100 degrees Fahrenheit for long periods may cause birth defects or miscarriage. If you are pregnant, contact your doctor for advice before trying a hot soak.

Invest in a new mattress. A soft, sagging mattress may contribute to the development of back problems or worsen an existing problem. If a new mattress is not in your budget, however, a three-quarter-inch-thick piece of plywood placed between the mattress and box spring can help a little. In addition, try to sleep on your back with two pillows propping up your knees.

Relax. Much back pain is the result of muscles made tight by emotional tension. Learn and practice a relaxation technique, such as meditation, or try a deep-breathing exercise, such as closing your eyes, breathing slowly and deeply, and counting backward from 100.

Preventing Future Pain

Many of the activities you engage in each day, such as sitting, lifting, bending, and carrying, can put a strain on your back. You can help prevent pain and ensure the health of your back for years to come by learning new ways of doing these things.

Use a cushion. Most seats in cars and trucks are not designed to support the small of your back, although some newer vehicles do provide adjustable lumbar support, at least for the driver. If the seat in your vehicle doesn't, buy a small cushion that can be fitted to provide the missing support. Despite what your mother told you about sitting up straight, leaning back at an angle of about 110 degrees is ideal for the back. If you sit for long hours, get up and walk around periodically to increase blood flow and decrease stiffness.

Put your arm behind your back. If you get stuck sitting for a long period in a seat that doesn't support your lower back and you don't have a cushion, try rolling up a towel or sweater so it has about the same circumference as your forearm. Then slide the rolled-up cloth between your lower back and the back of the seat. In a pinch, you can simply slide your forearm between your lower back and the seat back to ease the strain on your back. Try to make small adjustments in the curvature of your lower back every few minutes or so.

Swim. Many experts agree that swimming is the best aerobic exercise for a bad back. Doing laps in the pool can help tone and strengthen the muscles of the back and abdomen, which help support the spine, while buoyancy temporarily relieves them of the job of holding up your weight. Walking is the next best choice.

Lift with your knees bent. The large muscles of your legs and buttocks are better equipped to bear heavy weight than your back muscles are. Keep your back straight and bend only your knees, rather than bending at the waist, as you squat to pick up something. Then, as you rise, concentrate on using your leg muscles to push your upper body and the object back up into a standing position, again without bending at the waist.

Carry objects close to your body. When picking up and carrying heavy objects, pull in your elbows and hold the object close to your body. When reaching for a bulky item on a shelf, stand beneath it and rest the object on your head. That way your erect spine carries the weight, placing less burden on your back muscles.

Headaches

If you suffer from frequent, severe headaches that put you out of commission several times a month, you need to seek medical attention. Likewise, if your headaches are associated with physical exertion; changes in vision; or weakness, numbness, or paralysis of the limbs, skip the urge to self-treat and see a doctor. If you're already seeing a physician and aren't getting relief, think about getting a referral to a headache specialist or headache clinic. However, if you get only the occasional headache, read on.

Lie down. Lying down and closing your eyes for 30 minutes or more might be one of the best treatments for a bad headache. For some types of headaches, such as migraines, rest may be the only way to interrupt the pain cycle.

Don't let the sun shine in. Resting in a darkened room may alleviate the pain, especially if your symptoms resemble those of a migraine (severe pain on one side of the head, nausea, blurred vision, and extreme sensitivity to light). Bright light may also cause headaches. Even staring at a glowing computer screen may be enough to trigger brain pain. Wearing tinted glasses or using other means to filter bright light and minimize glare might keep away headaches.

Use a cold compress. A washcloth dipped in ice-cold water and placed over the eyes or an ice pack placed on the site of the pain are other good ways of relieving a headache. Whatever you use, keep in mind that speed is critical: Using ice as soon as possible after the onset of the headache will relieve the pain within 20 minutes for most people.

Try heat. If ice feels uncomfortable to you, or if it doesn't help your headache, try placing a warm washcloth over your eyes or on the site of the pain. Leave the compress on for half an hour, rewarming it as necessary.

Quit smoking. Smoking may bring on or worsen a headache, especially if you suffer from cluster headaches—extremely painful headaches that last from 5 to 20 minutes and come in groups.

Don't drink. Drinking more alcohol than you're used to often causes a pounding headache. But even a single serving of some alcoholic beverages can trigger headaches in certain people. For example, dark alcoholic beverages, such as red wines, sherry, brandy, scotch, vermouth, and some beers, contain large amounts of tyramine, an amino acid that can spark headaches in people who are sensitive to it.

Get moving. Regular exercise helps release the physical and emotional tension that may lead to headaches. Walking, jogging, and other aerobic activities help boost the body's production of endorphins (natural pain-relieving substances).

Cut down on caffeine. The same chemical in coffee and tea that perks you up in the morning can also make your muscles tense and raise your anxiety level. Consuming too much caffeine can also cause insomnia, which can trigger headaches. Another problem is that many people drink several cups of coffee a day during their workweek but cut their consumption on Saturdays and Sundays. This pattern can lead to weekend caffeine-withdrawal headaches.

Muscle Pain

Muscle soreness and cramps aren't generally life threatening, but they can be uncomfortable and painful. They can also dim your enthusiasm for physical activity, which in turn can negatively affect your overall health and well-being. Here are some tips to ease the pain and prevent the problem from recurring.

Stop. If your muscle cramps up while you're exercising, *stop*. Don't try to "run through" a cramp. Doing so increases your chance of seriously injuring the muscle.

Give it a stretch and squeeze. When you get a cramp, stretch the cramped muscle with one hand while you gently knead and squeeze the center of the muscle with the fingers of the other hand. Try to feel how it's con-tracted, and stretch it in the opposite direction.

Walk it out. Once an acute cramp passes, don't start exercising heav-ily right away. Instead, walk for a few minutes to get the blood flow-ing back into the muscles.

Try quinine. Many competitive swimmers drink tonic water, which gets its flavor from a small amount of qui-nine, to prevent cramps. Although there isn't much in the way of scientific research to support drinking tonic water for muscle cramps, you might want to try it.

Go bananas. Muscle cramps can sometimes be caused by a lack of potassium. Try eating a banana a day—the potassium-rich fruit might help keep cramps away.

Chill out. If you know you've overworked your muscles, immediately take a cold shower or a cold bath to reduce the trauma to them. World-class Australian runner Jack

Foster used to hose off his legs with cold water after a hard run. He told skeptics if it was good enough for race-horses, it was good enough for him! If an icy dip seems too much for you, ice packs work well, too. Apply cold packs for 20 to 30 minutes at a time every hour for the first 24 to 72 hours after the activity (just place a thin cloth between the ice pack and your skin). Cold helps prevent muscle soreness by constricting the blood vessels, which reduces blood flow and thus inflammation.

Avoid heat. Using heat may feel good, but it's the worst thing for sore muscles because it dilates blood vessels and increases circulation to the area, which in turn leads to more swelling. Heat can actually increase muscle soreness and stiffness, especially if applied during the first 24 hours after the strenuous activity.

Drink plenty of fluids. One cause of acute cramps, especially when you're exercising intensely during hot weather for an hour or longer, is dehydration. Be sure to drink enough fluids before, during, and after exercising. If you're running, aim to drink about a cup per hour. Don't overdo it, however, because drinking too much water can cause a dangerous imbalance in the body's mineral stores.

What about those sports drinks? You really don't need them unless you're exercising intensely for longer than an hour at a time. Water is better.

GUT REACTIONS

Digestive difficulty got you down?
Although most problems in the
gastrointestinal tract are minor,
a few are extremely uncomfortable and may even be
embarrassing. Eating is considered one of life's simple
pleasures—it shouldn't make you uncomfortable.
But don't worry: Constipation, diarrhea, heartburn,
lactose intolerance, and nausea and vomiting don't
have to interfere with your eating enjoyment. Relief
may be closer than you think.

Constipation

Irregularity is one of those things that no one likes to
talk about. It's personal and, well, a little awkward. But
if you have ever been constipated, you know it can put
a real damper on your day. A sudden change in bowel
habits requires a visit to your doctor to rule out more
serious underlying problems. But for the occasional
bout of constipation, here are some tips to put you back
on track.

Get moving. When you are active, so are your bowels—
and the more sedentary you are, the more slowly your
bowels move. That may partially explain why older

people—who tend to be less active—and those who are bedridden are prone to becoming constipated. You don't have to run a marathon; a simple walking work-out will do.

Raise your glass. Drinking an adequate amount of liquid may help alleviate constipation or prevent it from happening in the first place. The reason for this is simple: If you are dehydrated, your stool will become dry and difficult to pass. A good rule of thumb is to drink a total of six to eight cups of fluid throughout the day, and perhaps a bit more when you're perspiring heavily during exercise or hot weather. (This general guide doesn't apply, however, if you have a kidney or liver problem or any other medical condition that restricts your intake of fluid. In that case, your doctor will need to advise you on how much fluid is appropriate.)

The caffeine in a cup of coffee can stimulate the bowels, so a cup or two of java (or tea) in the morning might help get things moving. But because caffeine is also a diuretic that pulls fluid out of your body, be sure to fill most of your fluid needs with water, seltzer, juice, milk, or decaffeinated beverages.

Bulk up. Sometimes, a little extra dietary fiber is all you need to ensure regularity. Fiber, the indigestible parts of plant foods, adds mass to the stool and stimulates the colon to push things along. Fiber is found naturally in fruits, vegetables, grains, and beans (although refining and processing can significantly decrease their fiber content). The current recommendations for daily dietary fiber intake are 20 to 35 grams, but most people eat only 10 to 15 grams a day.

Eat at least five servings of fruits and vegetables daily. Select a variety of fruits and vegetables, and opt for the fresh produce over juice as much as possible. A glass of orange juice, for instance, provides 0.1 gram of fiber, while eating an orange gives you 2.9 grams.

Eat six ounces of grain products each day. That's in addition to the five servings of fruits and vegetables just mentioned. Grain products include cereals, breads, and starchy vegetables (such as corn, green peas, potatoes, and lima beans). Whenever possible, choose whole grains such as whole-wheat bread and whole-grain cereal. Check the labels on cereal boxes; anything with more than five or six grams of fiber per serving qualifies as high fiber. The best bread has at least two grams of fiber per slice and is labeled "whole-grain" or "whole-wheat" (the word "wheat" alone or a brown color does not guarantee that the product includes the whole grain). And don't forget beans. Dried beans and legumes are excellent sources of fiber.

Reject refined foods. Bump up your fiber intake by switching from refined foods to less-refined foods whenever possible. Switch from a highly processed cereal to a whole-grain cereal, move from heavily cooked vegetables to less-cooked vegetables, and choose whole-grain products over products made with white flour. A half-cup serving of white rice has 0.3 gram of fiber; a half-cup serving of brown rice contains 1.75 grams. And while a one-ounce serving of potato chips has 1.2 grams of fiber, a one-ounce serving of popcorn supplies 4.1 grams.

Diarrhea

Diarrhea is uncomfortable and unpleasant, but generally no big deal in otherwise healthy adults. However, if diarrhea becomes a chronic condition, the situation changes. Or if it affects the very young, the elderly, or the chronically ill, it can be dangerous. And if you don't drink enough fluids, you could find yourself complicating what should have been a simple situation.

Unless diarrhea persists—which can signal a more serious problem—you usually don't find out its cause. Treatment for a temporary bout is aimed at easing the symptoms and at preventing dehydration, the most serious consequence of diarrhea.

Hello, Doctor?

See a doctor for your diarrhea if

- You see blood in your stool.
- You experience symptoms of dehydration, including dizziness when you stand up, scanty and deep-yellow urine, increased thirst, and dry skin. Children may also cry without producing tears.
- You have a fever or shaking chills.
- The diarrhea persists for more than 48 to 72 hours.
- The person with diarrhea is very young, very old, or chronically ill.

Keep hydrated. You can lose a lot of liquid in diarrhea, but you also lose electrolytes, which are minerals such as sodium and potassium that are critical in the running of your body. Drink two quarts (8 cups) of fluids a day, three quarts (12 cups) if you have a fever. Plain water lacks electrolytes, but it's a good, gentle-on-the-tummy option that can help you replace lost fluid. Other choices include weak tea with a little sugar; sports drinks, such as Gatorade; flat soda pop (decaffeinated flavors like ginger ale are best); and fruit juices other than apple and prune, which have a laxative effect. Another option is to buy an over-the-counter electrolyte-replacement formula, such as Pedialyte, Rehydralyte, or Ricelyte. These formulas contain fluids and minerals in the proper proportion.

Whatever you choose to drink, keep it cool, not ice cold. And sip, don't guzzle—small amounts at a time will be easier on your insides.

 **Sip some broth.** Any broth flavor will do, but drink it lukewarm instead of hot, and add a little salt to it if it's not already salty.

Put a heating pad on your belly. It may help relieve abdominal cramps.

Try yogurt. Choose a brand that contains live lacto-bacillus cultures, which are friendly bugs that normally live in the gut. (Even people with lactose intolerance can usually handle this type of yogurt.)

Eat easy-to-digest foods. Good choices include soup, gelatin, rice, noodles, bananas, potatoes, toast, cooked carrots, soda crackers, and skinless white-meat chicken.

Don't do dairy. Avoid milk, cheese, and other dairy products (except yogurt, unless you don't usually toler-ate it well) while you have diarrhea, as well as for one to three weeks after it stops. The small intestine, where milk is digested, is affected by diarrhea and simply won't work as well for a while.

Cut out caffeine. Just as it stimulates your nervous sys-tem, caffeine jump-starts your intestines. And that's the last thing you need when you have diarrhea.

Say no to sweet treats. High concentrations of sugar can increase diarrhea. The sugar in fruit can do the same.

Steer clear of greasy or high-fiber foods. These are harder for your gut to handle when you have diarrhea.

Heartburn

Your esophagus, the tube that carries what you swallow down to your stomach, can literally be burned by the industrial-strength acids your stomach releases to digest food. Those acids are meant to stay where the tough stomach lining can handle them. Unfortunately, we can experience something called reflux. That's when some of the stomach contents, including the acid, slip back up through the esophageal sphincter, the valve that's supposed to prevent the stomach's contents from reversing course. The reflux causes that burning sensation between the stomach and the neck. Here are some ways to put out that fire and keep it from flaring up again.

Keep your head up. One way to protect your esophagus while you sleep is to elevate the head of your bed. That way, you'll be sleeping on a slope, and gravity will keep your stomach contents where they belong. Put wooden blocks under the legs at the head of your bed to raise it about six inches.

Is It Really Heartburn?

If symptoms don't subside, you may have something other than a simple case of heartburn. The symptoms of more serious illnesses, such as heart disease, can mimic those of heartburn. And if it is heartburn, it may be caused by a hiatal hernia (in which part of the stomach slips up into the chest cavity), inflammation of the esophagus, ulcers in the stomach or small intestine, or even cancer. So if you're still suffering even after following the self-help advice here, see your doctor.

Say no to a postdinner snooze. People who lie down with a full stomach are asking for trouble. Wait at least an hour before you lie down.

Loosen your belt. Tight clothing can push on your stomach and contribute to reflux.

Lose the fat. Abdominal fat pressing against the stomach can force the contents back up.

Get in shape. Even mild exercise done on a regular basis, such as a daily walk around the neighborhood, may help ease digestive woes. However, avoid working out strenuously immediately after a meal; wait a couple of hours.

Don't smoke. Nicotine from cigarette smoke irritates the stomach lining, as well as the valve between the stomach and the esophagus, so smokers tend to get heartburn more often.

Be careful of coffee. The caffeine in coffee relaxes the esophageal sphincter, which can lead to reflux. But even decaffeinated coffee may cause reflux problems: Research suggests the oils contained in both regular and decaffeinated java may play a role in heartburn. Experiment to see if cutting your coffee intake lessens your heartburn.

Be wary of peppermint. For some people, peppermint seems to cause heartburn. Try avoiding the after-dinner mints and see if it helps.

Skip the cocktail. Alcohol can relax the sphincter and irritate the stomach, which can lead to reflux.

Slow down on soda. The carbon dioxide in soda pop and other bubbly drinks can cause stomach distention, which can push the contents of the stomach up into the esophagus.

Lactose Intolerance

Eating dairy products has unpleasant consequences for 30 million to 50 million Americans because they're lactose intolerant. That means they don't properly digest lactose, the sugar found in all milk products. This problem is usually due to a shortage of the enzyme

Hidden Sources of Lactose

Lactose lurks in many prepared foods, so check labels carefully. Bread, cereals, pancakes, chocolate, soups, puddings, salad dressings, sherbet, instant cocoa mix, candies, frozen dinners, cookie mixes, and hot dogs may all contain lactose. Although the amounts of lactose may be small, people with low tolerance levels can experience symptoms from them.

When perusing ingredient labels, it's not just milk that you have to watch for. Whey, curds, milk by-products, dry milk solids, nonfat dry milk powder, casein, galactose, skim milk powder, milk sugar, and whey protein concentrate are all words that indicate the presence of lactose.

lactase, which breaks down milk sugar in the small intestine into simple parts that can be absorbed into the bloodstream. The end result of this lactase deficiency may be gas, stomach pains, bloating, and diarrhea. If you're lactose intolerant, you may want to try these helpful tips to ease your symptoms.

Determine your level of lactose intolerance. The best way to assess your tolerance is to first get all lactose out of your system by avoiding lactose-containing foods for three to four weeks. Then start with very small quantities of milk or cheese. Monitor your symptoms to see how much or how little dairy food you can handle without experiencing discomfort. Once you know your limits, management becomes easier.

Stick with small servings. Although you may not be able to tolerate an eight-ounce glass of milk all at once, you may have no discomfort from drinking a third of it in the morning, a third of it in the afternoon, and a third of it at night.

Pair your dairy. If you eat some cheese or drink a little milk, plan to do so with a meal or a snack. Eating dairy on an empty stomach can worsen your symptoms.

Try yogurt. Yogurt with active cultures doesn't cause problems for many lactose-intolerant people, but you may have to buy it at a health-food store. Yogurt is a great source of calcium, if you can tolerate it.

Choose hard cheeses. If you can't pull yourself away from the cheese aisle, pick hard, aged cheeses, such as Swiss, cheddar, or Colby. They contain less lactose than soft cheeses.

Get calcium from other foods. Lactose-intolerant people, especially women and children, should be sure their calcium intake doesn't plunge. Green leafy vegetables, such as collard greens, kale, turnip greens, and Chinese cabbage (bok choy), as well as oysters, sardines, canned salmon with the bones, and tofu provide lots of calcium, as does calcium-fortified orange juice and soy milk. You may also want to take calcium supplements; talk with your doctor about the dosage that is right for you.

Watch out for medications. Lactose is used as filler in more than 20 percent of prescription drugs (including many types of birth control pills) and in about 6 percent of over-the-counter medicines. If you take such a medication every day, it could cause symptoms. Complicating matters is the fact that lactose may not be listed under the inactive ingredients on the label. Ask your doctor or pharmacist, or contact the drug's manufacturer to find out if what you're taking contains lactose.

Nausea & Vomiting

We've all been there, and it's no fun. Perhaps it's the "24-hour flu" bug, or maybe it was something you ate.

Whatever the cause, now you're feeling queasy and sick. The tips that follow are designed to reduce your discomfort and help relieve symptoms as quickly as possible, but if vomiting is violent or persists for more than 24 hours, or if your vomit contains blood or looks like coffee grounds, see a physician right away.

Let it run its course. The best cure for the 24-hour "stomach flu" (it isn't truly influenza; that's an upper respiratory infection caused by specific viruses) is bed rest and time. The more rest you get, the more energy your body will have to devote to fighting the invader.

Stick to clear liquids. If your stomach is upset, it probably doesn't need the additional burden of digesting food. Stick to fluids until you feel a little better and have stopped vomiting. Clear, room-temperature liquids, such as water or diluted noncitrus fruit juices, are easier to digest, and they are also necessary to prevent the dehydration that may result from vomiting or diarrhea.

Don't drink alcohol. Alcohol can be very irritating to the stomach, so if your tummy is turning over, now is certainly not the time to imbibe. You'll also want to avoid fatty foods, highly seasoned foods, beverages containing caffeine, and cigarettes.

Eat easy-to-digest foods. When you are ready to start eating again, start with soft, plain foods, such as bread, unbuttered toast, steamed fish, or bananas. Avoid fatty foods and foods that are high in fiber. Another tip is to start with tiny amounts of food and slowly build up to full meals.

Let it flow. The worst thing you can do for vomiting is fight it, because vomiting is your body's way of getting rid of something that is causing harm to your stomach. Plus, trying to hold back the urge can actually tear your esophagus.

Try a cold compress. A cold compress on your head can be very comforting when you are vomiting. It won't stop you from spewing, but it might help you feel a little better.

Balance those electrolytes. Along with replacing the fluids you lose through vomiting, it is also important to maintain the balance of sodium and potassium (the electrolytes) in your system. If you spend more than a day or two vomiting, have a sports drink, such as Gatorade, which is easy on the stomach and is designed to replace electrolytes. Try diluting it with water if drinking it straight bothers your stomach.

BREATHING BLOCKADES

True love or sky-diving may take your breath away, but otherwise, you don't want anything to inhibit your breathing. Your body is performing many important functions simultaneously, and they all need oxygen to work. When breathing isn't comfortable because of asthma, bronchitis, sinusitis, or even snoring, you won't be at your best. If you are facing one of these four conditions, try the following suggestions to keep your air about you.

Asthma

Some 20 million Americans have asthma, a condition in which breathing becomes difficult because of narrowing or blockage of the airways in the lungs. The lungs of people with asthma are inflamed and supersensitive; they're easily provoked into constriction by a wide variety of outside factors called triggers.

There are two main forms of asthma—allergic and nonallergic—with the allergic form being more common. Allergic asthma develops in people who have allergies, and the same substances (called allergens) that provoke their allergy symptoms also trigger their asthma symptoms. Both the allergy and asthma symptoms are the product of an overreaction by the immune system. Common triggers include dust mites, pollen, mold, and pet dander.

With nonallergic asthma, on the other hand, the triggers that irritate the lungs and bring on asthma symptoms have nothing to do with allergies or the immune system. This type of asthma can be sparked by dry air, cold weather, exercise, smoke, strong perfume, stressful situations, intense emotions, even laughing.

Although there is no cure for asthma, it can be managed. In addition to working with your doctor, you can take measures to help control the condition. The key is to track down your triggers and, as completely as possible, eliminate them from your life. In short, you can often help counter an asthma attack before it happens.

Smite the mite. Dust mites—or rather the feces and dead bodies of these microscopic bugs—are one of the most common allergic asthma triggers. They're everywhere in your home, although they love the bedroom because they feed on the dead skin cells we constantly shed, and we spend a great deal of time there. Reducing the number of dust mites will help ease symptoms if you have allergic asthma triggered by these little critters. Here are some tips (find more in the Allergies profile on page 5):

- Enclose your mattress in an airtight cover, and then cover it with a washable mattress pad.

- Wash your sheets in hot water every week, and wash your mattress pads and synthetic blankets every two weeks.

- Use polyester or Dacron pillows, not those made of kapok or feathers, and enclose them in airtight dust covers.

- Wear a mask over your mouth and nose while cleaning, and leave the room when you have finished the job.

Minimize mold. No matter how vigilantly you clean, mold and other forms of fungi are probably lurking somewhere in your house. To keep this stuff out, shut your windows, because mold spores can come right in, even if the windows have screens. In addition, stay out of attics, basements, and other dank, musty places; put on a face mask and check your bathroom (especially under the sink and in the backs of cabinets) and closet (especially unused shoes) for mold; and have someone else investigate the inner workings of air conditioners, humidifiers, and vaporizers for mold.

Make peace with pollen. Because it's just about impossible to escape pollen, learn how to control your exposure to the powdery allergen instead. Avoid cutting grass or even being outside while grass is being mowed. Keep your windows closed as much as possible and use an air conditioner to cool your home in warm weather. Room air purifiers are also available that can purify recirculated air, removing particles of all sorts. After being outside in the midst of pollen, take off your clothes and wash them, if possible, or run a vacuum over those that can't be washed. Wash yourself, too, including your hair.

Don't pet a pet. Taking a few commonsense measures may allow you to coexist with a beloved animal companion and its dander—the dead, dry skin that flakes off and triggers asthma symptoms. Never allow your pet into the bedroom: If the animal is in the bedroom at any time during the day, the dander will remain for hours. Leave the pet home if you are going for a car ride, and if you do have direct contact with your pet (or any animal), wash your hands right away. In addition, try bathing your dog or cat once every other week in warm water with no soap.

Bathing the animal in this way significantly reduces the amount of allergen on your pet's fur.

Watch the weather. Pay attention to how changes in the weather affect your asthma. You might even keep an asthma journal by recording the temperature, wind velocity, barometric pressure, and  humidity on days when you suffer attacks. Knowing what types of weather conditions can leave you gasping for air may help you avoid problems. For instance, people with asthma should stay indoors when it is very cold outside, because a rush of cold air can cause a spasm in the bronchial tubes.

Exercise your options. For years, people with asthma were told to avoid exercise because it would induce attacks. Research has shown, however, that getting regular aerobic exercise increases the amount of huffing and puffing an asthmatic can tolerate. Begin with short workouts and gradually increase their duration. Keep a bronchodilator with you, at least at first. If you feel tightness in your chest and can't work through it, use the device. If one type of exercise still brings on attacks, try another form of exercise. You may not be able to tolerate running, for example, but you may be able to swim regularly. Talk with your doctor about what will work best for you.

Avoid aspirin. Aspirin can trigger asthma attacks in certain people. Play it safe and avoid aspirin and products that contain it if you have asthma, even if you've never experienced a related flare-up. Check the labels on every over-the-counter drug you purchase. Avoid those that list "aspirin" and those that contain the initials "ASA," "APC," or "PAC"; ask the pharmacist if you are unsure whether the medication you want to buy contains aspirin.

According to a report from the National Asthma Education Program, people with asthma should also stay away from certain nonsteroidal anti-inflammatory agents (ibuprofen is one such medication) that have effects similar to aspirin's. Opt instead for such "usually safe alternatives" as acetaminophen, sodium salicylate, or disalcid, but check with your doctor to be sure. You may also need to avoid tartrazine (yellow food dye No. 5), which is found in a number of soft drinks, cake mixes, candies, and some medications, if it aggravates your asthma.

Mind your mind. The notion that asthma is "all in your head" has gone the way of many medical myths. However, doctors believe that asthma is an illness with both physical and emotional aspects. For example, asthma attacks can be triggered by emotional changes, such as laughing or crying, or by stress. Although you may not be able to "think away" an asthma attack, keeping your mind at ease may prevent you from panicking at the onset of an asthma attack, which will make a bout with breathing trouble less scary. A positive attitude works wonders to enhance your other coping methods.

Bronchitis

Bronchitis is an often-painful infection in the major bronchial tubes (airways) that lead to the lungs. A persistent virus, frequently the same one that causes colds or the flu, is most often the cause of acute bronchitis (rarely, bronchitis can be traced to a bacterium or fungus). Bronchitis causes the walls that line the inside of the bronchial tubes to swell and produce greatly increased amounts of thick yellow or green mucus. The lung irritation and mucus trigger a throaty, persistent, productive hacking, and the throat gets irritated from coughing. Other symptoms include a burning or aching pain just beneath the breastbone, a feeling of tightness in the chest, wheezing or shortness of breath, and/or a "rattling" sensation in the lungs and chest. A low-grade fever, chills, and achiness may also occur. The irritation caused by the virus in turn leaves the respiratory tract vulnerable to other complications, such as pneumonia.

Fortunately, acute bronchitis generally goes away on its own within a few days or a week, although the cough can sometimes linger for weeks or even months. Until your body has shaken the infection, however, there are some things you can do to decrease discomfort and help your body heal.

Humidify your environment. Believe it or not, coughing is actually good for you. It's the body's way of eliminating the infection that causes bronchitis. Help it along by using a warm- or cool-mist humidifier to add moisture to the air. The added humidity will help bring the sputum up and out of the body. Standing in a steamy shower with the bathroom door closed or keeping a pan of water at a slow boil on the stove (never leave it unattended!) can also help loosen and bring up phlegm.

Drink plenty of liquids. Taking in extra liquids helps keep the sputum more fluid and therefore easier to expel. It doesn't really matter what type of liquid you take in, although tea, soup, and other warm liquids may feel better than cold ones. As a bonus, warm fluids can also soothe the irritated throat that might result from all that coughing.

Gargle with warm salt water. Gargling with salt water may provide a double dose of relief by soothing the inflammation in the throat and by cutting through some of the gunky mucus that might be coating and irritating the sensitive throat membranes. However, watch your measurements. It only takes one teaspoon of salt in a glass of warm water; too much salt causes burning in the throat, and too little is ineffective. Gargle as often as you need to, but be sure to spit out the salty water after gargling.

Take aspirin or ibuprofen to relieve the chest pain. If a bout with bronchitis produces muscle pain in the chest, these anti-inflammatory medications may provide some relief. Aceta-minophen does not have an anti-inflammatory effect and so may be less helpful. However, because of the risk of deadly reaction called Reye's syndrome, don't give aspirin to children younger than 19; use acetaminophen instead.

Sinusitis

Inside your nose is an intricate system of narrow passages and eight hollow, air-containing spaces that enable you to inhale air from the environment and process it along to your lungs. The hollow spaces, known as the paranasal sinuses, are located in pairs behind the eyebrows, in each cheekbone, behind the nose, and between the eyes. The main function of your sinuses is as a "conditioner" for inhaled air on its way to your lungs. Normally, the membranes lining the nose and sinuses produce between a pint and a quart of mucus and secretions a day. This discharge passes through the nose, sweeping and washing the membranes and picking up dust particles, bacteria, and other air pollutants along the way. The mucus is then swept backward into the throat by tiny undulating hairs called cilia. From there, it is swallowed into the stomach, where acids destroy dangerous bacteria.

But when those nasal passages become irritated or inflamed by an allergy attack, air pollution, smoke, or a viral infection such as a cold or the flu, the nose and sinus membranes secrete more than the normal amount of mucus. They also swell, blocking the openings and preventing an easy flow of mucus and air. This sets the stage for bacteria to flourish. If your sinuses make your life miserable, you don't have to live with the discomfort.

Take good care of yourself. Maintaining a healthy immune system will bolster your resistance to germs, leaving you less likely to catch a cold or come down with the flu and making the symptoms more manageable if you do get sick. Shore up your body's defenses by eating right, staying in shape, and getting plenty of rest.

Live the sanitary life. You don't have to move into a sterile, germ-proof bubble or walk around wearing a surgical mask. Just use common sense: If the guy next to you at the bus stop is coughing his brains out, move away. And if someone in your family has a cold or the flu, avoid unnecessary contact with his or her germs.

Hydrate. Keeping yourself well-hydrated helps ensure your sinuses are in top shape. So drink plenty of fluids—eight tall glasses of water a day is a good goal.

Clear the air. Avoid pollutants in the air, stay indoors if the air quality is poor, and above all, avoid anyone who is smoking (and you should definitely not smoke).

Control allergies. Because allergies can cause sinusitis, know your allergy triggers and do your best to avoid them. (See the Allergies profile on page 5 for tips on avoiding allergens.) You can also see an allergist to investigate desensitization treatments designed to help the body develop immunity to the offending substance.

Snoring

Snoring (making a raspy, rattling, snorting sound while you breathe during sleep) is a fairly common affliction, affecting 40 percent of men and 25 percent of women. Older people are particularly prone to snoring: About one-third of people aged 55 to 84 snore. Snoring is a breathing and sleep disorder that can have serious medical consequences and may be a result of sleep apnea, a serious condition where breathing stops repeatedly during sleep. Sleep apnea also raises the risk of cardio-vascular disease (visit the National Sleep Foundation at www.sleepfoundation.org or speak with your doctor for more information). The tips that follow may help you—and your bed partner—sleep more peacefully.

Sleep on your side. You're more likely to snore if you're lying on your back, and sleeping on your stomach is stressful for your neck.

Use tennis balls. Not to shove in your mouth, but to keep you from rolling onto your back during sleep. Sew a long, tight pocket onto the back of your pajama top, and put two or three tennis balls into it. (Don't sew? Put the tennis balls in a sock and then use a safety pin to both close the sock and attach it to the back of your pajama top.)

Avoid alcohol and tranquilizers. Both alcohol and sleeping pills can depress your central nervous system and relax the muscles of your throat and jaw, making snoring more likely. These substances are also known to contribute to sleep apnea. (You should never, of course, drink alcohol and take tranquilizers at the same time.)

Lose weight. Excess body weight, especially around the neck, puts pressure on the airway, causing it to partially collapse.

Treat your allergies. Chronic respiratory allergies may cause snoring by forcing sufferers to breathe through their mouths while they sleep. Taking an antihistamine just before bedtime may help. If your nose is stuffed up, try using an over-the-counter saline spray or a humidifier. (See the Allergies profile on page 5 for more tips.)

Buy a mouth guard. Your dentist or doctor may be able to prescribe an antisnoring mouth guard that holds the teeth together and keeps the lower jaw muscles from becoming too lax.

See a doctor if you are pregnant and snoring. Sometimes, being pregnant will cause women to snore. The snoring may begin because of the increased body weight and because the hormonal changes of pregnancy cause muscles to relax. Whatever the reason, snoring during pregnancy can rob your baby of oxygen. Talk with your doctor about it.

Elevate your head. Sleeping with your head raised may take some of the pressure off the airway, making breathing easier. Raise the head of the bed by putting blocks under the bedposts, or prop up your upper body (not just your head, which can actually inhibit breathing) with pillows.

ON THE OUTSIDE

The skin is your body's largest organ, so it stands to reason there are a lot of things that can go wrong with it. The skin is also the body's most visible organ; as a result, when you have a problem somewhere on your surface, it feels as though everyone can see it. Skin issues run the gamut from minor annoyances to major diseases, so if you're ever in doubt about your epidermis, see a doctor. But there are simple remedies for blisters, stings, sun-burns, warts, and even psoriasis that can help you love the skin you're in.

Blisters

Blisters are tender spots that fill up with fluid released by tiny blood vessels in an area where delicate skin tissues have been burned, pinched, or just plain irritated. The feet are extremely susceptible to these small, yet painful problems. Virtually everyone has experienced friction blisters, the kind caused by hot, sweaty feet and/or ill-fitting shoes. If you're tiptoeing around a blister right now, read on to learn how to take care of it.

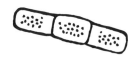 **Make a tent.** Instead of simply placing an adhesive bandage right on top of the blister, "tent" the bandage by bringing in its sides so the padding in the middle of the bandage raises up a bit. A tented bandage will help protect the blister while exposing it to air, which will speed healing.

Or, just let it breathe. Some physicians believe a blister needs as much exposure to air as possible and should never be covered. You may want to give your blister a chance to "breathe" occasionally by going without a bandage, especially when you're at home and your blister is less likely to need protection from bumps and debris.

Put it up. Elevating the blistered area can help relieve pressure and temporarily ease discomfort.

Drain it. Although some doctors believe a blister should never be popped because of the risk of infection, most agree that a blister causing extreme discomfort—such as one on a toe or under a nail—is a candidate for draining. However, you should never open a blister that was caused by a burn, and you should allow a doctor to treat a large blister that might open on its own through normal activity. If you want to pop a blister, first wipe the blister and a sewing needle with rubbing alcohol. Prick the blister once or twice near its edge, then slowly and gently press out its fluid.

Keep the roof on. Once you have popped the blister and drained the fluid, do not remove the deflated top skin. This skin, called the blister's roof, protects the blister from infection and forms a "bridge" across which new cells can migrate on their journey to heal the site.

Soak first. It will be much easier to drain a blister on a tough-skinned area, such as the sole of the foot, if you spend a day or two softening it up. Soak the blister for 15 minutes three or four times a day in Burow's solution, which is available at most pharmacies (follow package directions).

Watch for signs of infection. Visit your doctor if you see redness, red streaks, or pus around a blister.

Be patient. It usually takes about a week to ten days for the body to reabsorb the blister's fluid.

Psoriasis

Psoriasis is a noncontagious, chronic skin condition that produces round, dry, scaly patches that are covered with white, gray, or silver-white scales. These patches are called plaques. Although psoriasis is a mysterious condition (doctors aren't exactly sure what causes it or why it can be mild one day and serious the next), it is common. According to information from the National Institutes of Health, between 5.8 million and 7.5 million Americans have the disease. Psoriasis is also tough to treat because what works for one person may not work for another, and treatments that were once effective for an individual often become ineffective, and vice versa. Still, the following tips and your doctor's advice may help you show off your skin to the world.

Kitchen Solutions

You can make many anti-itch remedies right in your own kitchen. The National Psoriasis Foundation suggests the following recipes

• Dissolve 1½ cups baking soda in 3 gallons water to use in an anti-itch compress.

• Add a handful of Epsom salts or Dead Sea salts to your bathwater. You can also add a squirt of mineral oil or baby oil to the water with the salts (but be careful you don't slip in the tub).

• Put 3 tablespoons boric acid (available in pharmacies) in 16 ounces water, and use in a compress.

• Add 2 teaspoons olive oil to a large glass of milk for a soothing bath oil (but, again, be careful you don't slip in the tub).

• Add 1 cup white vinegar to the bathwater to ease itching.

• Soak in oats. Toss a cup of oats in your bathwater, or add a commercial bath product that contains "colloidal oats."

Get out in the sun. Although doctors want most of their patients to avoid the sun to prevent skin cancer and wrinkles, many people with psoriasis are encouraged to seek the sun's ultraviolet (UV) light, because the rays often cause psoriasis to clear. Doctors aren't exactly sure how sunlight works to heal psoriasis, but it seems to slow skin cell replication, the cause of those dry, scaly patches of skin. However, limit your time under the sun because a sunburn can cause the disease to flare.

The National Psoriasis Foundation suggests applying a thin layer of mineral oil to the affected areas to enhance the sun's effects and to keep the skin moist. The oil will also increase your sunburn risk however, so don't stay out too long. You should also cover unaffected areas of skin with sunscreen that has a sun protection factor (SPF) of at least 15; apply it 20 to 30 minutes before you go outside.

Try a vinegar dip. Apple cider vinegar has a long history of being used to soothe minor burns and other skin inflammations, and it's also a disinfectant. It's a great soak for affected fingernails and toenails; just pour some in a bowl or cup and dip your nails in for a few minutes. Some people have also had success applying it to plaques using cotton balls.

Beat the tar out of it. Tar-containing shampoos, creams, and bath additives can help loosen psoriasis scales. Tar-containing bath oils are especially beneficial for psoriasis that is widespread.

Pass the warm olive oil. If psoriasis scales are a problem on your scalp, warm a little olive oil and gently massage it into the scales to help soften and remove them. Then shampoo as usual and rinse thoroughly.

Humidify. Dry indoor air is associated with dry skin, which is bad news for people with psoriasis. Plug in a room humidifier to raise the humidity.

Stings

You hear the buzz, you see the bee, but before you can act—Oweee! You've been stung. Almost all of us have had this experience at least once, and it's no fun. But you can take the ouch out of being stung. For more than 2 million people in the United States who are allergic to the venom of stinging insects, however, consequences can be much worse than a little pain. Their symptoms can include hives, wheezing, dizziness, and nausea and require emergency medical treatment. In the worst cases, shock, unconsciousness, and cardiac arrest can occur. Those who don't have such serious reactions can try the following tips to take the soreness out of a sting.

Apply meat tenderizer. Simply applying a teaspoon of unseasoned meat tenderizer mixed with a few drops of water to a sting can bring quick relief. An enzyme in the tenderizer, either papain or bromelain, dissolves the toxins the insect just shot into you. Carry a bottle filled with the solution with you when you know you're going to be in an area with bees, because it only works when you immediately apply it to a sting.

Try a baking-soda paste. Think of this as "plan B" if you don't have any meat tenderizer. Although baking soda can't neutralize insect venom, it will help relieve itching and swelling.

Scrape out the stinger. Bees and some yellow jackets have barbed stingers that anchor in your skin after you're stung. (Other stinging insects have smooth stingers that remain intact on the bug.) You should get the stinger out as soon as possible because it will continue to release venom into your skin for several minutes after the initial sting. Resist the urge to squeeze, grab, or press the stinger, however. This will just make matters worse by pumping more venom into your skin. Try this instead: Using a clean knife blade, or even a fingernail, lift the stinger up and gently scrape it away.

Put it on ice. Rub ice over the sting site. This may help reduce some of the inflammation and swelling.

Sunburns

People have worshipped the sun for thousands of years, but only in the past century have humans worshipped the sun by intentionally baking them- selves to a golden tan or, as may be more often the case, an angry red burn beneath it. Although few things can penetrate the skin's outer layer (stratum corneum), the sun's ultravio- let rays easily pass through this protective envelope and damage the cells and structures beneath. A tan devel- ops because pigment-producing cells called melano- cytes produce brown pigment (melanin) to protect the skin from invading rays and prevent further damage to the skin's structures. Dark-skinned people more readily produce melanin, while light-skinned individuals don't produce it well or produce it in blotches that appear as freckles. This latter group burn easily, even with mild sun exposure.

Despite the dangers the sun poses, many of us are lax about protecting our skin. If you end up with a painful sunburn, the following remedies can help ease the pain. Keep in mind, though, that these remedies cannot reverse the damage caused by unprotected exposure to the sun's rays, damage that can lead to skin cancer. The best protection is to stay out of the sun.

Apply cool compresses. Soak a washcloth in cool water and apply it directly to the burned areas (do not put ice or an ice pack on sunburned skin) for several minutes, rewetting the cloth often to keep it cool. You can also add a soothing ingredient, such as baking soda or oatmeal, to the compress water. Simply shake a bit of baking soda into the water before soaking the cloth. Or wrap dry oatmeal in cheesecloth or a piece of gauze and run water through it. Then toss out the oatmeal and soak the compress in the oatmeal-water solution.

Take a soak. Slipping into a tub of chilly water is a good way to cool the burn and ease the sting, especially if the burn is widespread or on a hard-to-reach  area (such as your back). Avoid soap, which can irritate and dry the skin. If you feel you must use soap, use a mild one, such as Dove or Aveeno, and rinse it off well. Definitely skip the washcloth, bath sponge, and loofah.

Afterward, pat your skin gently with a soft towel. If you're usually tempted to linger in the tub for hours, take a shower instead. Soaking too long can cause or aggravate dry skin, which can increase itching and peeling.

Toss in some oatmeal. Adding oatmeal or baking soda to bathwater may help soothe skin even more than applying a compress or just soaking in plain water. Prepare the oatmeal as you would for an oatmeal compress, holding the bundle under the faucet as the tub fills, or buy Aveeno oatmeal powder at your local pharmacy or health-food store and follow the package directions. If you use baking soda, sprinkle it liberally into the water. Soak no longer than 15 to 20 minutes to avoid overdrying the skin.

Drink up. You can easily become dehydrated when you are sunburned. Drink plenty of fluids, especially water, like you would if you had a fever. You can determine whether you're hydrated enough with a quick check in the bathroom: If your urine is relatively clear, you're doing fine. If it's dark, you need to drink more water.

Warts
Most people have one of these ugly bumps at one point or another. Warts are caused by the human papilloma

virus (HPV) and are contagious. That's why an initial wart can create a host of others. Common warts are the rough-looking lesions most often found on the hands and fingers. The much smaller, smoother flat warts can also be found on the hands but might show up on the face, too. Warts that occur on the soles of the feet are called plantar warts and can sometimes be as large as a quarter. Genital warts, which have become a more common problem, develop in the genital and anal areas. If you suspect that you have a genital wart, see your doctor; do not try the remedies suggested here.

No one knows why warts occur and disappear and later recur in what appears to be a spontaneous fashion. For example, some women say they develop warts when they become pregnant, but the gnarly lumps disappear soon after they have their babies. A medical mystery also surrounds the fact that researchers have yet to find a way to get rid of warts for good. The solution may lie in developing a wart vaccine, but an approved, safe vaccine has yet to be created. That leaves the wart sufferer with two options: Having a dermatologist treat the warts or trying a few methods on their own. As for home remedies, some people swear by certain tactics, while others will never have any success with them. And it seems that in some cases, prevention may be the best medicine. Here are some tips to help you be wart-free.

Be sure it's a wart. First and foremost, before you try any type of treatment, know whether your skin eruption is a wart or another condition. Warts (except the small, smooth flat wart) commonly have a broken surface filled with tiny red dots. Moles, on the other hand, are usually smooth, regularly shaped bumps that are not flesh colored (as flat warts can be). A rough and tough patch that has the lines of the skin running through it may be a corn or a callus. There is also a chance that the lesion is skin cancer. You may be able to recognize skin cancer by its irregular borders and colors. But if you have any doubt, ask your doctor. In addition, if you have diabetes, circulation problems, or impaired immunity, do not try any home therapy for wart removal; see your doctor.

Don't touch. The wart virus can spread from you to others, and you can also keep reinfecting yourself. The virus develops into a wart by first finding its way into a scratch in the skin's surface—a cut or a hangnail, for instance. Even shaving can spread the flat warts on the face. Inadvertently cutting a wart as you trim your cuti-

Can You Wish Away Your Warts?

Some dermatologists agree that the power of suggestion, especially when used on children, can be very effective in making warts disappear. It may be that the warts were about to vanish anyway (children's warts usually disappear more quickly than warts in adults), or perhaps positive thoughts boost the immune system. No one knows for sure.

Taking the power of suggestion one step further, there have been studies of the use of hypnosis in the treatment of warts. For many people, the very word hypnosis conjures up images of a Houdini-type magician gently swaying a crystal bauble in the face of an unwilling suspect who, unbeknownst to him, is about to reveal the truth—or cluck like a chicken. Unlike popular myth, hypnosis cannot make you do something you don't want to do. Today, it is an accepted way to quit smoking and can even be helpful with weight loss.

In one study, 17 people with warts were treated with hypnosis once a week for five weeks. Seven other patients were not treated with hypnosis. Both groups were asked to abstain from any wart treatment, including home remedies. The patients who underwent hypnosis were told that they would experience a tingling sensation in the warts on one side of their body and only those warts would disappear. Nine patients lost more than three-quarters of all their warts, and four of them lost all the warts on both sides of their body. Meanwhile, the untreated group showed no improvement. It's not clear why the patients who underwent hypnosis had better luck getting rid of warts, but it's possible that the power of suggestion strengthened their immune systems, which defend against viruses.

cles can cause an infection. So keep viral travels to a minimum by not touching your warts at all, if possible. If you do come in contact with the lesions, thoroughly wash your hands with soap and hot water.

Stick to it. An effective treatment for warts that's cheap and doesn't leave scars is adhesive tape. In fact, a 2002 study found that tape therapy eliminated warts about 85 percent of the time, compared to a standard medical treatment using liquid nitrogen, which was only successful on 60 percent of warts. Wrap the wart with four layers of tape. Be sure the wrap is snug but not too tight. Leave the tape on for six-and-a-half days, and then remove the tape for half a day. You may need to repeat the procedure for about three to four weeks before the wart disappears. You can try this on a plantar wart, but be sure to use strips of tape that are long enough to be properly secured.

Try castor oil. The acid in castor oil probably does the trick by irritating the wart. It works best on small, flat warts on the face and on the back of the hands. Apply castor oil to the wart with a cotton swab twice a day.

"C" what you can do. Vitamin C is mildly acidic, so it may irritate the wart enough to make it go away. Apply a paste made of crushed vitamin C tablets and water. Apply the paste only to the wart, not to the surrounding skin. Then cover the area with gauze and tape.

Heat it up. One study found that having patients soak their plantar warts in very hot water was helpful because it softens the wart and may kill the virus. Be sure the water is not hot enough to cause burns, however.

Don't go barefoot. Warts shed viral particles by the millions, so going shoeless puts you at risk for acquiring a plantar wart. The best protection is footwear. Locker rooms, pools, public or shared showers, even the carpets in hotel rooms harbor a host of germs—not just wart viruses. You can catch any of a number of infections, from scabies to herpes simplex. Never go barefoot; at the very least, wear a pair of flip-flops.

Keep dry. Warts tend to flourish in an environment that's damp, especially in the case of plantar warts. That's why people who walk or exercise exten-sively may be more prone to foot warts, says the American Academy of Dermatology. So change your socks any time your feet get sweaty, and use a medicated foot powder to help keep them dry.

Cover your cuts and scrapes. The wart virus loves finding a good scratch so it can make its way under your skin. By keeping your cuts and scrapes covered, you'll help keep the wart virus out.

Take precautions with over-the-counter preparations.
The Food and Drug Administration (FDA) has approved wart-removal medications made with 60 percent salicylic acid, but most common over-the-counter remedies contain 17 percent. While the stronger formulas may work well for adults (except for those who have sensitive skin), they are not recommended for children. Salicylic acid works because it is an irritant, so no matter which strength of solution you use, try to keep it from irritating the surrounding skin. If you are using a liquid medication, do this by smearing a ring of petroleum jelly around the wart before using the medication. If you're applying a medicated wart pad or patch, cut it to the exact size and shape of the wart. Apply over-the-counter liquid medications before bed and leave the area uncovered.